Contents

Acknowledgements, vii
Introduction, ix

Chapter 1 – Couture, page 1

Its meaning and place in the fashion industry, 1 – Couture house organisation, 1 – Couture controlling and supporting bodies, 4 – International couture, 5 – Paris couture houses, 8 – London couture houses, 8 – Hollywood and haute couture, 12 – The decline of the couture system in the 1960s, 12 – The revival of couture in the 1980s and 1990s, 16 – Making techniques and their influence on fashion, 18 – Characteristics and specialities of fitters, 21 – Couture today, 21

Chapter 2 – Ready-to-Wear, page 23

Definition, 23 – Origins of ready-to-wear, 23 – The evolution of ready-to-wear, 26 – Utility Clothing, 27 – Fashion revolution in London in the 1960s, 27 – The influence of the 1960s revolution on Paris, 32 – Design process, 40 – Ready-to-wear manufacturing techniques, 40 – Ready-to-wear workrooms or studios, 40 – Factors in the growth of the ready-to-wear industry, 41 – The regulating or supporting bodies, 41 – Ready-to-wear versus haute couture, 42 – The Japanese influence, 43 – The emergence of Belgium, 43 – Italy's role in ready-to-wear, 44 – British ready-to-wear, 44 – America: the first in ready-to-wear, 44

Chapter 3 – Mass Production, page 49

The mass production process, 49 – Production, 52 – Sizing, 56 – Design strategies in mass production, 56 – Lines within a design house, 56 – Offshore production, 59 – Ethical trading, 59 – New trends, 60

Chapter 4 – Tailoring, page 61

History, 61 – Male-dominated craft, 61 – Bespoke tailoring, 61 – Savile Row, 63 – The supremacy of the English tailors, 64 – Royal patronage and influence, 64 – The ethos of English tailoring, 65 – Specialist tailors, 67 – Tailoring techniques, 68 – The bespoke tailoring process, 71 – Tailoring cloth suppliers, 71 – Couture tailoring, 74

Chapter 5 – Menswear, page 77

Definition of menswear (wholesale tailoring), 77 – The British tradition, 77 – Tailoring for the masses, 77 – The middle market, 79 – The effect of market forces on manufacturing, 80 – Specialist, patented and branded items, 82 – America, 82 – The Italian influence, 86 – Menswear and the 1960s fashion revolution, 87 – Designer menswear, 87 – Itinerant tailors and the rag trade, 87 – Men's ready-to-wear today, 90

Chapter 6 – Dressmaking, page 93

The origins of dressmaking, 93 – Dressmaking as part of traditional female education, 93 – Dressmaking as a career, 94 – Paper patterns, 94 – Levels of dressmaking, 99 – The difference between the dress industry and the dressmakers' craft, 100

Chapter 7 – Millinery and Accessories, page 101

The couturiers' ancillary trades, 101 – Millinery, 101 – Paris milliners, 105 – The millinery manufacturing process, 108 – The decline of the milliner, 108 – Buttons, 110 – Belts, 111 – Shoes, 112 – Embroiderers, 112 – Pleaters, buttonholers and pressers, 114 – Linings and interlinings, 114

Chapter 8 – The Designers, page 116

A minister of fashion and an official designer to the Revolution, 116 – The father of haute couture, 118 – The tailored suit for women, 118 – New styles for a new century: the extravagant and the classic, 120 – Three powerful women: Chanel, Vionnet and Schiaparelli, 121 – Two opposing forces: the New Look and free form, 124 – The genius of the second half of the 20th century, 126 – Casual classicism, 128 – New York style, 129 – The Sixties, 130 – New couture, 134 – The renegades: James, Gaultier and Westwood, 135 – Italian high life and glamour, 136 – Italian couture today, 138 – A new tailoring, 139 – The Italian ready-to-wear designers, 139 – The impact of the Japanese, 140 – The Belgian force, 142 – American simplicity, 143 – An Austrian and German duo, 143 – All change, 143

Chapter 9 – Distribution, page 145

Distribution, 145 – Buying and selecting, 145 – Marketing, 146 – Merchandising, 147 – Advertising, 147 – Display, 149 – Selling strategies, 149 – Corporate management, 150 – Mail order, 151 – Department stores, 151 – Other retail outlets, 155

Chapter 10 – Fashion Organisation and Calendar, page 157

The press, 157 – Public relations, 158 – Fashion forecasting, 158 – The fashion stylist, 163 – The fashion educators – fashion schools, 163 – Recruitment agencies, 165 – Models and model agencies, 165 – The fashion calendar, 166

Chapter 11 – Considerations for the Future, page 173

Government initiatives, 173 – Financial backing, 173 – The need for a fully integrated computer-aided system, 173 – Plagiarism, 174 – Can couture survive? 174

Appendix I – The Incorporated Society of London Fashion Designers (Britain), page 175

Appendix II – The Chambre Syndicale de la Couture Parisienne (France), page 178

Organisation, 178 – Aims, 178 – Organised events abroad, 178 – French cultural and promotional events, 179 – Press promotion, 179 – Public relations, 179 – Defence of artistic copyright, 179 – Vocational training, 179